DID YOU HEAR THAT?
HANDWRITTEN POEMS

REALITY IS NOT EXISTENCE

DA CHASE

MYSTERY WATERS

MASTER DECIPHER

BAD HABITS

A LOVER'S NOTE

UNNOTICED

CHASING COTTON CANDY

PREDETERMINED

NONAMENODATE.MP

VISIBLE TEARS

SHIMES

Dauntrel Alfred Finn

REALITY IS NOT EXISTENCE
_2022_

WE KEEP GETTING CAUGHT AT THE SEAMS.
SEEING WE WERE FABRICATED ON DIFFERENT FABRICS OF THE UNIVERSE,
SHE WAS SPACE & TIME HAD TO BE ME.
A GOLDEN THREAD OF IMMORTALITY WAS OUR CONNECTION.
CLOTHED BY REINCARNATION SO WE COULD FEEL THE WARMTH OF FOREVER,
TIME HAS NO DISCRETION.
FORBIDDEN LOVE IS THE TH CARDINAL SIN
I THINK KONG WAS JUST THE STORY OF THE FALL OF MEN.
AND SHE,
WAS THE BEAUTY THAT KILLED THE BEAST.
YOU CANNOT SAVE A MONSTER.
BUT SHE IS THE HEAVEN I AM DYING TO SEE,
SO I WOULD DIE AT HER FEAT.
WE FOUND EXISTENCE IN THE MOMENTS IN BETWEEN SECONDS—
WHERE REALITY IS JUST A BLUR,
EVERY CONVERSATION IS LESSONED
AND SILENCE IS VERSED.
WHERE SILENCE IS COMFORT.
SHE MAKES AN EVIL ME FEEL GOOD.
I AMPLIFY HER LIGHT AS ALL DARKNESS SHOULD.
I WOULD LOVE FOR NIGHT TO LAST FOREVER,
BUT SOMETIMES I KNOW THE DAZE MUST GET HER.

We keep gettin caught of the senses.
Seeing we were fabricated on different fabrics of the universe,
She was space and time had to be me.
A golden thread of immortality was our connection.
Clothed by reincarnation so we could feel the warmth of forever,
Time has no discretion.
Forbidden is like the 8th cardinal sin,
I think Kong was just the story of the fall of man
        love
And she,
Was the beauty that killed the beast.
You cannot save a monster.
But she is the heaven I am dying to see.
So I would die at her feet.
We found existence in the moments
In between seconds —
where reality is just a blur,
Every conversation is
lessoned,
And silence is versed.
Where silence is comfort.
She makes an evil me feel good.
I amplify her light
as all darkness
shall.
I would live for
night to last
forever.
But sometimes I
know the daze must
get her...

REALITY IS NOT EXISTENCE

daChase
2021

I CAN TELL YOU'RE SACRED, BABY.
YOU ARE MAGIC AND THERE IS SORCERY IN MY HANDS—
YOU ARE A FORCE TO UNDERSTAND,
CAN I EXPLORE WHERE YOU EXPAND?
AND...
I CAN TELL YOU'RE NAKED, BABY,
EVEN WITH YOUR CLOTHES ON.
TRANSPARENCY IS A SIGN OF THE DIVINE
AND AT THE CHANCE THAT WE ALIGN
EVEN IF ONLY FOR ONE CONVERSATION ONE TIME.
I'D HOPE THAT WE COULD FALL OUT OF THE STRINGS OF REALITY
AND THRU DIMENSIONS
WHERE TIME LACKS EXISTENCE
AND THERE ARE ONLY LINEAR COMPOSITIONS OF WHAT WE COULD BE.
YOU ARE THE PEYOTE TO MY MESCALINE,
THE DIVINE TO MY FEMININE.
I AM THE PSYCHEDELIC MASCULINE WITH HORNS THAT COULD MATCH YOUR SIN...
I AM FREEDOM OF THE SOUL AND YOU MUST BE THE PLACE THEY ROAM ONCE FREE.

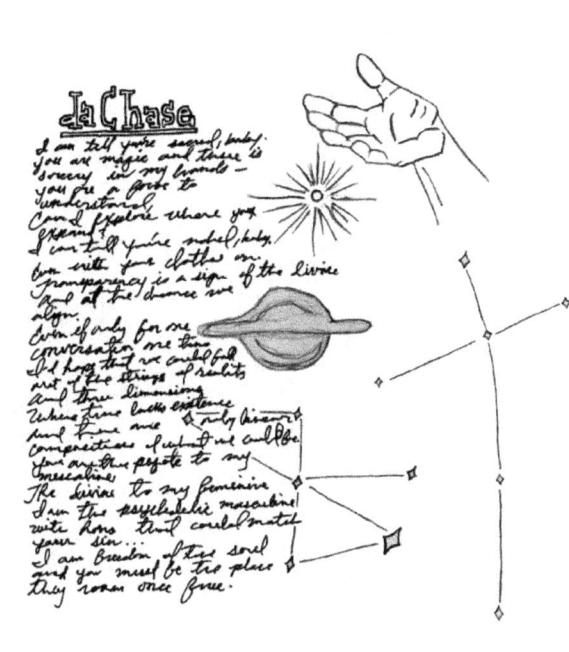

da Chase

I can tell you're sacred, baby,
you are magic and there is
sorcery in my bones —
you are a probe to
understand
can I explore where you
I can tell you're naked, baby,
even with your clothes on.
Transparency is a sign of the divine
And at the chance we
align,
Even if only for one
conversation, one time
I'd hope that we could find
out of the strings of reality
and three dimensions
where time lacks existence
And free me & only disarm
connections of what we could be
You are the peyote to my
mescaline
The divine to my feminine
I am the psychedelic masculine
with love that could match
your sin...
I am freedom of the soul
and you must be the place
they roam once free.

MYSTERY WATERS
2022

IF I COULD SIPHON OFF THE BREATH GOD INHALED TO BREATHE INTO EVE-
I KNOW IT'S A LITTLE DIRT ON MY LUNGS BECAUSE I'VE BEEN SMOKING SINCE I WAS   -
I WOULD CAUSE A TORNADO INTO THE DUST AND LUST OUT THE BODY THAT IS YOU.
YOUR ENERGY SPEAKS TO ME LIKE SCRIPTURE.
THE HIGHS YOU OFFER ARE THE TOUCH OF GOD'S MERCY.
I'M SURE THE VOICES IN MY HEAD SCREAMING TO CHASE YOU ARE MY DISCIPLES, JUDAS BEING THE LOUDEST, YES
BUT CRUCIFIXION DOESN'T BRING ME FEAR IF YOU'RE THE HEAVEN REVERED TO MY DEMISE.
OH, YOU MUSE ME.
OH... YOU...
TOUCH LIFE INTO A MAN WHO HAS SEEN THE EYES OF MEDUSA.
IF CURIOSITY KILLS THE KITTEN, MAY I KISS LIFE BACK INTO YOURS?
EXCUSE ME IF I'M TOO FORWARD BUT THE PAST HAS NEVER DONE MUCH FOR ME BUT TENSE,
I JUST WANTED TO RELAX A BIT, LOVE.
CAN I REST IN YOUR ENERGY?
CAN I REST IN YOUR PEACE?
BECAUSE TO THE GRAVE, I'LL CHASE YOUR GRAVITY.
THROUGH PLANES, I'LL TEETER YOUR DIMENSIONS.
MON AMI.
CAN I TREAD IN THE MYSTERY OF YOUR WATERS?

Mystery Waters

if i could siphon
off the breath God inhaled
t' breathe into ore —
i know there's a little dirt on my
lungs, i've been smoking since i was 16 —
i would cause a tornado into the dirt and
rost out the body that it you, like scripture.
your energy speaks to me of God's mercy.
the highs you offer the touch of God's mercy.
I'm sure the voices in my head screaming
to chase you are my disciples,
Judas being the loudest, yes.
But crucifixion doesn't bring me fear
if yours the heaven revered to my
demise.
oh, you muse me.
oh... you...
touch life into a man who has seen the
eyes of Medusa.
if curiosity kills the kitten may i kiss life
back into yours?
excuse it if i'm too forward but the past
has never done much but tease,
i just wanted to relax a bit, love.

Can i rest in your energy?
Can i rest in your peace?
Because the grave will chase your gravity.
through Hades, i'll tether your dimensions.
Kingdom;
Can i tread the mystery of your waters?

<u>MASTER DECIPHER</u>
2019

MY GRANDFATHER DIED IN THE ARMS OF THE SPIRIT OF HIS MOTHER.
TOO MUCH COCAINE IN HIS VEINS TO SUSTAIN.
I WAS BORN IN THE SAME VOID HE LEFT.
I KNOW PAIN BY THE POUND BY THE SAME VOICE THAT KEPT THE OPPRESSED SATIATED.
IT WAS WICKED WHEN THE WISE TURNED WISDOM TO A WEAPON,
BUT I GUESS IT'S THE SAME PLANE THAT TURNS KARMA TO A LESSON.
LEST CONSEQUENCE BE NONSEQUENTIAL LIKE—
DAMN, A NIGGA CAN'T DO SHIT.
INTEGRITY IS THE WEAK MAN'S JUSTIFICATION.
I WAS BORN BY THE RIVER WHERE IT ENDS AT THE LAKE.
I WAS FORCED INTO SHIVERS BY THE COLD OF THE HATE.
I SHARE BLOOD WITH MORE DEMONS THAN SATAN—
DROWNED WITH NO WATER,
I WAS CHANGED BY THE SHRINE MEANT TO ALTER.
SACRIFICED AS AN OFFER.
PEACE WAS ONLY SOMETHING MY HEART KNEW.
IT BROKE WHEN I WAS YOUNG.
I JUST NEVER TRIED TO PUT IT BACK TOGETHER 'CAUSE I HAVEN'T BEEN MERRY SINCE
HUMPTY DUMPTY STORIESSSS.....

MY GRANDFATHER DIED IN THE NAME OF THE SPIRIT OF HIS MOTHER.
THE MUSIC CRAWLED IN HIS VEINS TO SUSTAIN
I WAS BORN IN THE SAME VOID HE LEFT.
KILLING PAIN BY THE AUDIO BY THE SAME VOICE THAT KEPT THE
OPPRESSED SATIATED.
IT WAS WICKED WHEN THE WISE TURNED WISDOM TO A
BETRAYAL
BUT I GUESS IT'S THE SAME FLAME THAT TURNS KARMA
TO A LEMON.
LEST CONSEQUENCE BE NON SEQUENTIAL LIFE—
DAMN, A NIGGA CAN'T DO SHIT.
INTEGRITY IS A WEAK MAN'S JUSTIFICATION.
I WAS BORN BY THE RIVER WHERE IT ENDS AT
THE LAKE.
I WAS FORCED INTO SHIVERS BY THE COLD
OF THE HATE.
I SHAKE HAND WITH MORE DEMONS
THAN SATAN—
DROWNED WITH NO WATER,
WAS CHANGED BY THE SHRINE
BEFORE ITS ALTER.
SACRIFICED AS AN OFFER.
PEACE WAS ONLY SOMETHING MY
HEART KNEW.
I BROKE WHEN I WAS YOUNG,
I JUST NEVER TRIED TO
PUT IT BACK TOGETHER
'CAUSE I HAVEN'T
BEEN MARRY SINCE HUMPTY
DUMPTY STORIES.

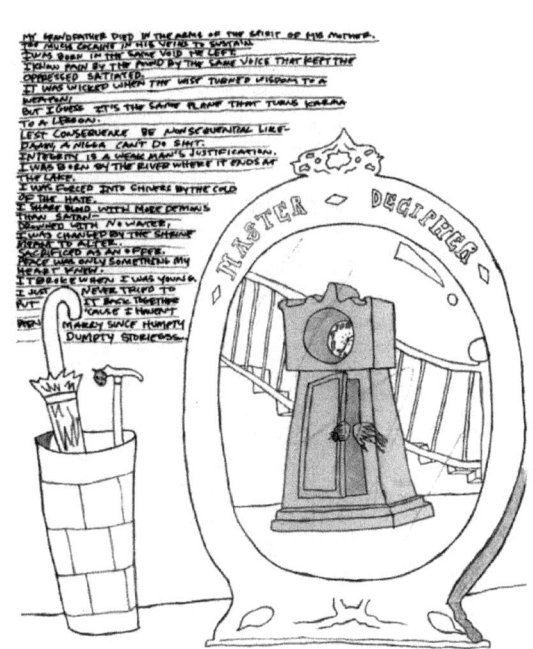

BAD HABITS
_2019_

I WAS RAISED ON BAD HABITS.
I CAN'T TELL THE DIFFERENCE BETWEEN SELF-DESTRUCTION & SELF-LOVE, OR
SELF-CARE AND SELFISHNESS.
HENNESSY LOOK LIKE HERBAL TEA WITH NO CREAMER.
SO A DRUNKEN ME FEELS THE MOST HEALTHY.
BROKEN HOMES MAKE BROKEN MINDS.
SOULS SOW SEEDS THAT GROW INTO TREES,
I HOPE WE SURVIVE.
TREES BREATHE OXYGEN BUT WE KEEP CHOPPIN' THEM.
BROKEN HOMES DON'T GET FIXED WE JUST BUILD NEW ONES TO BREAK.
WORSE THAN THAT WE WERE TAUGHT IF I HAD TO YOU HAVE TO.
IN A SAD TRUTH, YOU CAN'T HELP OTHERS UNTIL YOU HELP YOURSELF
WE WEREN'T TAUGHT HOW TO APOLOGIZE BUT TO REPENT TO SEE HEAVEN,
SO WELCOME TO HELL.
I WAS RAISED OFF FUCKIN' BAD HABITS.
ALL THAT UPBRINGING SEEMED TO ONLY BRING ME DOWN.
ALL THESE BAD HABITS.
ALL THAT FUCKIN' PREYING JUST SEEMED TO BRING ME CLOSER,
'CAUSE JESUS'S STORY WAS TRAGIC.
I GUESS THE ONLY WAY TO GLORY IS CRUCIFIXION.
SO I CROSS MY HEART AND FIX MY LIPS TO ASK WHO MATCHIN',
MY WHOLE EXISTENCE.
I WAS RAISED ON ALL THESE BAD HABITS.

I WAS RAISED ON BAD HABITS.
I CAN'T TELL THE DIFFERENCE BETWEEN SELF-DESTRUCTION & SELF-LOVE, OR SELF-CARE AND SELFISHNESS.
HENNESSY LOOK LIKE HERBALTEA WITH NO CREAMER.
SO A DRUNKEN ME FEELS THE MOST HEALTHY.
BROKEN HOMES MAKE BROKEN MINDS.
SOULS SOW SEEDS THAT GROW INTO TREES,
I HOPE WE SURVIVE.
TREES BREATHE OXYGEN BUT WE KEEP CHOPPIN' THEM.
BROKEN HOMES DON'T GET FIXED WE JUST BUILD NEW ONES TO BREAK.
WORSE THAN THAT WE WERE TAUGHT 'IF I HAD TO YOU HAVE TO'.
IN A SAD TRUTH, YOU CAN'T HELP OTHERS UNTIL YOU HELP YOURSELF.
WE WEREN'T TAUGHT HOW TO APOLOGIZE BUT TO REPENT TO SEE HEAVEN,
SO WELCOME TO HELL.
I WAS RAISED ON FUCKIN' BAD HABITS.
ALL THAT UP-BRINGING SEEMED TO ONLY BRING ME DOWN.
ALL THESE BAD HABITS.
ALL THAT FUCKIN' PREYING JUST SEEMED TO BRING ME CLOSURE.
'CAUSE JESUS STORY WAS TRAGIC.
I GUESS THE ONLY WAY TO GLORY IS CRUCIFIXION.
SO I CROSS MY HEART AND FIX MY LIPS TO ASK WHOS MATCHIN'.
MY WHOLE EXISTENCE.
I WAS RAISED ON ALL THESE BAD HABITS.

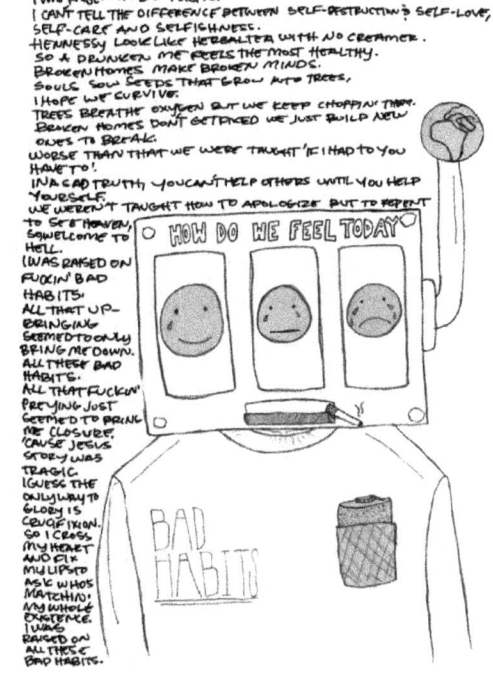

A LOVER'S NOTE
2021

PLAGUED WITH PEACE.
TRYING TO PIECE TOGETHER
SLIVERS OF SILVER LININGS.
HOPING TO BE DELIVERED
FROM WITHERED MINDINGS—
OVER MATTERS BUT THAT
ONLY WORKS WHEN WHAT
DON'T MATTER IS WHAT YOU
DON'T MIND.
NO WONDER MINE CAN'T
ELUDE THE THOUGHT OF YOU.
PLAGUED WITH PEACE.
CAN'T REALLY SHOW YOU WHERE
IT HURTS.
VAGUE RELIEFS OF SPONTANEITY,
MAKE YOU FEEL YOUNG AGAIN.
MAKE ME FEEL SUMN AGAIN.
A RAGE RELEASED—
WHAT I MUST BE BRUCE BANNER?
YO NEW PATTERN MAKES YOU
REFLECT A TRUE SATURN.
WHAT YOU MUST WANT A RING?
TELEPATHIC ANTICS.
EVEN MILES AWAY I HEAR YOU
CALLIN' ME.
I'M PLAGUED WITH PEACE.
LEAST WITH YOU, THO,
I GOT ALL MY PIECES.

PLAGUED W/ PEACE.
TRYING TO PIECE TOGETHER SLIVERS OF SILVER LININGS.
HOPING TO BE DELIVERED FROM WITHERED MINDINGS-
OVER MATTERS BUT THAT ONLY WORKS WHEN WHAT
DON'T MATTER IS WHAT YOU DON'T MIND.
NO WONDER MINE CAN'T ELUDE THE THOUGHT OF YOU.
PLAGUED W/ PEACE.
CAN'T REALLY SHOW YOU WHERE IT HURTS.
VAGUE RELIEFS OF SPONTANEITY,
MAKE YOU FEEL YOUNG AGAIN.
MAKE ME FEEL SUNN AGAIN.
A RAGE RELEASED—
WHAT I MUST BE BRUCE BANNER?
YO NEW PATTERN MAKES YOU REFLECT A
TRUE SATURN.
WHAT, YOU MUST WANT A RING?
TELEPATHIC ANTICS.
EVEN MILES AWAY I HEAR YOU CALLIN' ME.
I'M PLAGUED W/ PEACE.
LEAST WITH YOU I GOT
ALL MY PIECES.

A Lover's Note

UNNOTICED
2022

LIKE A LEAF IN A STREAM BETWEEN TREES OFF A TRAIL IN A FOREST THAT NO LONGER GETS VISITS.
LIKE DUST CARRIED IN A BREEZE.
LIKE SEDIMENT SETTLED AT THE BOTTOM OF BOTTOMLESS LAKES,
WHIRLPOOLS SPONTANEOUSLY OCCUR SACRIFICING SMALL INCREMENTS OF LIFE TO MOTHER NATURE,
EMBERS DYING OUT AT THE END OF WILDFIRES THAT WERE MISSED BY THE FIREMAN'S HOSE,
BABY BIRDS WHOSE WINGS COULDN'T CATCH WIND FOR FLIGHT WHO REST AT THE ROOTS OF TREES WHO HOMED THEM.
LIKE DISCARDED THOUGHTS SCRATCHED INTO BALLED-UP PAPERS NEAR THE MOUTHS OF TRASH BINS,
FORGOTTEN HEADPHONES ON DESKS IN ROOMS NEXT TO ASSIGNMENTS UNDONE BUT ARE DUE,
LOST BOXES IN ATTICS AND GARAGES OF HOARDED TRINKETS OF INSIGNIFICANT SENTIMENT,
CRUMBS UNDER COUCHES THAT ARE ONLY APPETIZING TO STARVING BELLIES.
LIKE UNSPOKEN WORDS CAUGHT IN THE THROATS BY THE COLD CLAWS OF ANXIETY.
THIS PAIN I CARRY MAY ALWAYS GO UNNOTICED.

CHASING COTTON CANDY
2022

MRS. THERAPY
IS IT THE LITTLE BOY SITTING OUTSIDE HIS MOTHER'S DOOR HOPING SHE WILL AT LEAST MAKE EYE CONTACT WHEN SHE COMES OUT?
BECAUSE SHE WON'T EVEN COME OUT UNTIL THE MORNING.
OR THE BOY ON THE FRONT PORCH WITH A PACKED BAG AND BINOCULARS SEARCHING UP THE ROAD FOR HIS DAD WITH EAGERNESS IN HIS EYES?
BECAUSE HE NEVER ARRIVES.
IS IT THE KID WHO CREEPS DOWN THE STAIRS EARLY ON CHRISTMAS TO SEE MOM DIDN'T SECRETLY MAKE US BELIEVE WE WOULD BE GIFTLESS FOR A GREATER SURPRISE?
BECAUSE MOTHER NEVER LIES, THERE WERE NO PRESENTS.
IS IT THE KID SITTING ALONE NEAR THE PHONE WITH VOICES RINGING IN HIS EARS WAITING FOR HIS FATHER'S NAME TO APPEAR ON THE CALLER ID?
BECAUSE HE DOESN'T CALL UNTIL TOMORROW'S TOMORROW.
WHY DO I CHASE LOVES THAT NEED CHASERS?
WHY DO I CHASE LOVES I CAN ONLY FEEL THE BRIEF SENSATIONS JUST OUTSIDE THE GRASP OF MY FINGERTIPS?
WHY DO I CHASE LOVES I KNOW WILL NEVER LOVE ME BUT ONLY VALIDATE MY BELIEF THAT I CAN'T BE LOVED?
WHY DO I CHASE LOVE?
ISN'T THERE SOMEONE RIGHT HERE, AND READY?
IS THAT WHY I NEGLECT THEM?
IS THAT WHY MY EYES NEVER SETTLE DOWN WHEN THERE IS LOVE AT MY FEET?
MAYBE IT'S THE BOY WHO ONLY LET HIS PILLOW SEE HIS TEARS AND HIS PENCIL HEAR HIS VOICE.
MAYBE I LOVE CHASING COTTON CANDY.

Abs. Therapy:

Is it the little boy sitting outside his mother's door hoping she will at least make eye contact when she comes out? Because she won't even come out until morning.

Or the boy on the front porch with a packed bag and binoculars searching up the road for his dad with eagerness in his eyes?

Because he never arrives.

Is it the kid who creeps down the stairs early on Christmas to see mom didn't secretly make us believe we would be giftless for a greater surprise?

Because mother never lies, there were no presents.

Is it the kid sitting alone near the phone with voices ringing in his ears waiting for his father's name to appear on the caller ID?

Because he doesn't call until tomorrow's tomorrow.

Why do I chase loves that need chasers?

Why do I chase loves I can only feel the brief sensations of just outside the grasp of my fingertips?

Why do I chase loves I know will never love me but only validate my belief that I can't be loved?

Why do I chase love?

Isn't there someone right here, and ready?

Is that why I neglect them?

Is that why my eyes never settle down when there is love at my feet?

Maybe it's the boy who only let his pillow see his tears and his pencil hear his voice.

Maybe I love chasing cotton candy.

PREDETERMINED. (A LOVE LETTER FROM LIFE TO DEATH)

2021

HELLO FRIEND,
I ALWAYS MISS YOU UNTIL YOU RETURN.
I ALWAYS HATE YOU IN YOUR PRESENCE.
MIXED EMOTIONS, I GUESS BECAUSE I FEEL FIXED IN MOTION.
LIFE IS LINEAR,
DEATH IS WHEN YOU FINALLY REACH INFINITY.
I FEEL LIKE I'VE BEEN COUNTING FOR ETERNITY.
I FEEL LIKE TIME MAY END BEFORE NUMBERS DO.
EXISTENCE IS NOTHING ( ).
RECURRING IS BEYOND OUR CONTROL,
LIKE SNAILS IN LIFE'S GARDEN, WE JUST WANT A TASTE OF FRUIT.
YOU CAME BACK AS ROOT.
I KEEP RETURNING AS SOIL.
I WANTED TO BE A PLANT TOO, SO TURNOVER IS MY TURMOIL.
I REMAIN,
I PRAY YOU GET PLANTED AGAIN EVERY DAY.
AND WHEN THE SUN ISN'T OUT,
I FEAR YOU MAY WILT AWAY.
I WISH I WAS WATER & YOU NEEDED ME.
INSTEAD, YOU FEED FROM ME BUT SEEK A MIST OF CLEANSING.
I KEEP RETURNING AS SOIL & YOU HATE BEING DIRTY.
I ESCAPE BEING WORTHY.
YOU ARE HARVESTED AND GONE,
IT'S INNATE I AM DIRT DEEP.
YOU ARE PLANTED & BACK HOME,
MY LOVE FOR YOU IS PREDETERMINED.

HELLO FRIEND
I ALWAYS MISS YOU UNTIL YOU RETURN.
I ALWAYS HATE YOU IN YOUR PRESENCE.
MIXED EMOTIONS, I GUESS BECAUSE I FEEL FIXED IN MOTION.
LIFE IS LINEAR, DEATH IS WHEN YOU FINALLY REACH INFINITY.
I FEEL LIKE I'VE BEEN COUNTING FOR ETERNITY.
I FEEL LIKE TIME MAY END BEFORE NUMBERS DO.
EXISTENCE IS NOTHING (0).
RECURRING IS BEYOND OUR CONTROL,
LIKE SNAILS IN LIFE'S GARDEN, WE JUST WANT A TASTE OF FRUIT.
YOU CAME BACK AS ROOT.
I KEEP RETURNING AS SOIL.
I WANTED TO BE A PLANT TOO, SO TURN OVER IS MY TURMOIL.
I REMAIN.
I PRAY YOU GET PLANTED AGAIN EVERYDAY.
AND WHEN THE SUN ISN'T OUT,
I FEAR YOU MAY WILT AWAY.
I WISH I WAS WATER AND YOU NEEDED ME.
INSTEAD, YOU FEED FROM ME BUT SEEK A MIST OF CLEANSING.
I KEEP RETURNING AS SOIL AND YOU HATE BEING DIRTY.
I ESCAPE BEING WORTHY.
YOU ARE HARVESTED AND GONE,
IT'S INNATE I AM DIRT DEEP.
YOU ARE PLANTED AND BACK HOME,
MY LOVE FOR YOU IS PREDETERMED.

PREDETERMINED
A LOVE LETTER FROM LIFE TO DEATH

NONAMENODATE.MP
2020

WITH NO EXCUSE,
MY HEART BLEEDS
WHEN I BREATHE.
IT DOESN'T BEAT
WHEN I SLEEP.
I'M BEREAVED
AND I GRIEVE,
AS I SEEP
THRU THE SEAMS.
REALITY, AS IT
SEEMS, EVADES ME
AND I SCREAM,
BUT—
IF A NEGLECTED
CHILD SCREAM-CRIES
INTO HIS PILLOW
IN THE DEAD
OF NIGHT WHILE
EVERY ONE SLEEPS
DID HE EVEN
MAKE A SOUND?

With no excuse,
my heart bleeds
when I breathe.
It doesn't beat
when I sleep.
I'm bereaved
and I greive,
as I seep
thru the seams.
Reality, as it
seems, evades me
and I scream,
but—
If a neglected
child scream-cries
into his pillow
in the dead
of night while
every one sleeps
did he even
make a sound?

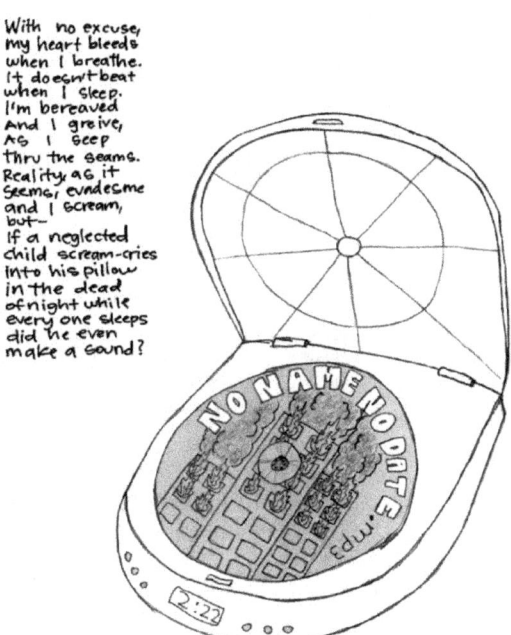

VISIBLE TEARS
2021

I DON'T CRY VISIBLE TEARS.
I CRY THE TYPE OF TEARS THAT LOOK LIKE TAKING   PILLS FOR A HEADACHE THAT REQUIRES TWO.
I CRY THE TYPE OF TEARS THAT LOOK LIKE ISOLATION WHEN I NEED A HUG. I DON'T KNOW HOW TO ACCEPT LOVE. I DON'T KNOW HOW TO TRUST BEING LOVED. LOVE HAD ALWAYS EQUATED TO PAIN FOR ME AND THE MORE YOU HURT, THE MORE YOU MUST BE GETTING LOVED UNTIL RESENTMENT LOOKS LIKE PASSIVE AGGRESSION MASKED BY APPRECIATION—
I DON'T CRY VISIBLE TEARS.
ALTHOUGH I WANT TO.
ALTHOUGH, I REALLY NEED TO. LEST I EXPLODE AND BLOOD VOMITS FROM MY MOUTH IN THE FORM OF ENRAGED YELLING AND SCARS APPEAR ON MY KNUCKLES FROM PUNCHING THE AIR. I WOULD JUST LIKE TO CRY, ALONE IN YOUR ARMS BUT DON'T ASK ME WHAT'S WRONG BECAUSE I SWEAR TO GOD, I'M OKAY. I NEED YOU TO LEAVE ME ALONE BUT STOP LEAVING ME ALONE SO MUCH. I NEED YOU TO UNDERSTAND THINGS I CAN'T EXPLAIN AND QUITE FRANKLY JUST DON'T WANT TO TALK ABOUT. OR EVEN THINK ABOUT FOR THAT MATTER.
I DON'T CRY VISIBLE TEARS ANYMORE.
JUST THE TYPE THAT PPL ONLY NOTICE WHEN IT'S TOO LATE.

i don't cry visible tears.
i cry the type that look like taking 13 pills for a headache that requires two.
i cry the type that look like when i know i need a hug. isolation
i don't know how to accept love. i don't know how to trust being loved. Love had always equated to pain for me and the more you hurt, the more you must be getting loved until resentment looks like passive aggression masked by appreciation.
i don't cry visible tears.
Although i want to.
Although, i really need to. Lest i explode and blood vomits from my mouth, in the form of enraged yelling and soaps appear on my knuckles from punching the air. i would just like to cry alone in your arms but don't ask me what's wrong because i swear to God, i'm okay. i need you to leave me alone but stop leaving me alone so me oh i need you to understand things i can't explain and i need you to quite frankly just don't want to talk about or even think about for that matter.
i don't cry any more.
Just the type that people only notice when it's too late.

VISIBLE TEARS

SHIMES
2022

SUBTLE SHAMES, SYNCHRONIZED HURTS, & HISTORIES.
HOME IS AN IDEA YOU LOVE, HOUSED IN SHROUDED MYSTERY.
I, FOR ONE, CAN SEE YOU. DO YOU SEE YOURSELF?
MAYBE I AM GOOD FOR ASSUMING, MY MIRRORED EYES WOULD LET YOU BE YOURSELF.
ENEMIES, AT TIMES, COME IN THE FORM OF INSECURITIES.
SOMEONE TOLD ME ONCE TRANSPARENCY WOULD BE MY PURITY.

SAVIORS ONLY COME WHEN IT'S TOO LATE SOMETIMES.
HONESTY IS NOTHING MORE THAN THE AUDACITY OF PEACE.
I, FOR ONE, FIND COMFORT IN THE DISPLACEMENT OF TIME.
MENTAL CAPACITIES GET SO FULL OVER THE LEAST.
EVERYTHING COULD JUST BE EVERYTHING, THAT'S FINE.
STRONGHOLD GUARDS AND PADDED WALLS WHERE WE ROAM FREE.

Subtle shames, synchronized hurts, & hysteries.
Home is an idea you love, housed in shrouded mystery.
I, for one, can see you. Do you see yourself?
Maybe I am good for assuming, my mirrored eyes
would let you be yourself.
Enemies, at times, come in forms of insecurities.
Someone told me once transparency would be my
purity.
    Savings only come when it's too late sometimes.
    Honesty is nothing more than the audacity of peace.
    I, for one, find comfort in the displacement of time.
    Mental capacities get so full over the least.
    Everything could just be everything, that's fine.
    Strong hold guards and padded walls where
      we roam free.

www.ingramcontent.com/pod-product-compliance
Lightning Source LLC
Chambersburg PA
CBHW061349040426
42444CB00011B/3156